I0236458

Roberto's

Laughterpedia of Fun Plus

STOCKWELL
PUBLISHERS SINCE 1898

Published in 2022 by
Roberto in association with
Arthur H Stockwell Ltd
West Wing Studios
Unit 166, The Mall
Luton, Bedfordshire
ahstockwell.co.uk

British Library Cataloguing-in-Publication Data
A catalogue record for this book is
available from the British Library.
ISBN: 9780722351642

*All characters appearing in this work are
fictitious. Any resemblance to real persons,
living or dead, is purely coincidental.*

Proceeds from the sale of this book will
be donated to the Dogs Trust

dogstrust.org.uk

Also from Roberto...

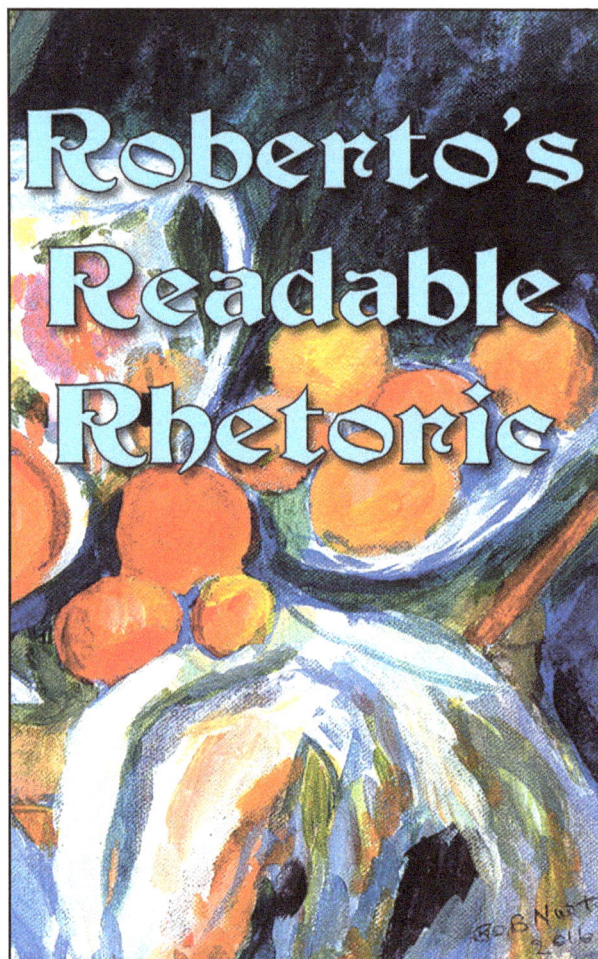

Introduction

More jokes, writings and paintings by an ordinary person for ordinary people.

Just smile, laugh and even say, "Ugh!" if it's what you want to do.

A smile does not hurt anybody.

A seventy-five-year-old man was sitting at a bar beside a young lady in a low-cut dress, looking at her.

He leaned towards her and said, "I say, what is keeping that dress on you?"

She replied, "Only your age!"

Did you know that the longest word in the English language is smiles, because there is a mile between the first and last letters!

What did Geronimo shout as he jumped off the cliff?
"Me!"

Why are there no aspirins in the jungle?
Because the paracetamol!

Who succeeded the first prime minister?
The second one!

DO YOU AGREE THE PAST IS OVER?

Did you hear about the man convicted of stealing luggage from the airport? He asked for twenty other cases to be taken into account.

An elderly man over eighty visits the doctor for an examination.

"How can I help you?" asks the Doctor.

"Well, I'm about to get married to a twenty-one-year-old and I want to be sure everything is OK."

After the examination, the Doctor says, "You are fine, but I would suggest that you may have certain problems at times, so I recommend you get a young companion for your wife."

"What a good idea!" says the man.

After a year they see each other again.

The Doctor says, "How are you?"

"I'm fine," says the man, "and my young wife is pregnant."

"So the companion worked?" asks the Doctor.

"Oh yes," says the man, "she's pregnant too!"

I used to have a fear of painting, but I brushed it off!

I CAME, I SAW, BUT DID NOT STAY VERY LONG.

An old plumber says to a young apprentice, "You have it easy these days. When I was learning they never turned the water off and made us keep ahead by laying two sections of pipe."

There are so many squirrels now. It should be possible to catch and cook them, but make sure you are not allergic to nuts.

What's the difference between roast beef and pea soup?
Anybody can roast beef.

A honeymoon couple arrive at their hotel.
The receptionist says, "Bridal?"
The bride blushes and says, "No, thanks – I'll hold on to his shoulders until I get the hang of it."

WHEN I FINALLY GOT MY HEAD TOGETHER MY BODY FELL APART.

At the golf club, a male streaker with a hood and mask runs through the ladies' changing room, in which three ladies are changing.

The first lady says, "It's not my husband."

The second lady says, "It's not my husband either."

The third lady says, "And he's not a member of this club."

President Trump was at an important meeting surrounded by terrific security.

A bodyguard noticed a sniper in a perfect position to assassinate him and called out, "Mickey Mouse!"

Another bodyguard said, "Why didn't you say 'Donald Duck'?"

How to keep your figure: keep an open mind and a closed refrigerator.

CONTENTMENT IS THE MOTHER OF INVENTION.

A guy out with his girlfriend at the weekend says, "I would like to buy you a diamond ring."

She chooses one priced at £2,000.

"No, no," he says. "Look at this one – £30,000."

She agrees and says, "OK!"

The guy pays by cheque, and the shopkeeper says, "It's fine, but you can't pick it up until Monday, when the cheque clears."

"OK," says the guy.

On the Monday the guy goes to the jeweller, who says, "Sorry – the cheque bounced!"

The guy says, "Don't worry – I had a great weekend!"

Paddy is dying.

He calls his two sons, wife and a solicitor to his bedside and says to his eldest son, "I'm leaving you the parade of shops in the High Street."

To his second son he says, "I'm leaving you the two large factories."

To his wife he says, "All the houses in Earl's Court and Queen Street are yours."

The solicitor says, "I didn't know he was involved in property; I thought he was a window cleaner."

IS A CHAMPAGNE HANGOVER THE WRATH OF GRAPES?

Two elderly ladies meet over the years for tea and cakes.

One day one lady says, "I'm terribly sorry, but I can't remember your name."

The second lady says, "When do you want to know by?"

A hairdresser always had to be better than his customer.

The customer said, "I've just bought a BMW and a house in St James Avenue, and I'm going to Rome to meet the Pope!"

The hairdresser said, "You should have bought a Jaguar and a home in Columbus Square. It is a much better area. As for meeting the Pope, I bet you £100 you don't meet the Pope and talk to him!"

Later, on his return, the hairdresser said, "I don't mind if you pay me by cheque."

"Oh no," the customer said, "the Pope actually spoke to me. He said, 'Where on earth did you get that haircut?' "

FOR A CHINESE DIET USE ONLY ONE CHOPSTICK.

Destiny

Chapter One

Redwood City was a bustling town situated in the county of Chipperford on the edges of the hills of Cade, which lead down to the desert of Heritage. The nearest settlement, Belsab, was nothing more than a single high street with a saloon and one or two rooming houses. Civilisation seemed to pass it by, and consequently it began to attract notorious characters who wished to evade the law. Its location was such that any rogue or outlaw could break the law without any bother, and moreover they knew there would be a kindly if expensive welcome from Slim Dachet, the renegade who not only acted as if he ran the town but he did.

It was into this hotbed of iniquity that Jed Cougan rode on a bright spring morning. Jed was a short, squat man, only about five feet six inches tall, and he was black. He had been brought up in the adjoining town of Rittlestone, where he had to fend for himself. This at times was not only difficult; it was nigh on impossible. So he lived by his wits and consequently became so fast and accurate with his six-guns that at times it frightened him, and the effect it had on the people of Rittlestone led to the usual business of being challenged to a gunfight by anybody, particularly when they had a few drinks. So Jed, for their safety and his own, decided to pack his bags and leave for pastures new.

He rode into Redwood City to the Renay Saloon, tethered his horse, pushed open the swing doors and swaggered to the bar.

"Give me a whisky, friend."

This was the word that would get him into many a scrap in the future.

"What the hell do you want in here?" said the barkeeper.

"Just bring me a bottle!"

"We are not allowed to serve Indians or blacks—"

He never finished the sentence. Jed grabbed him by the neck with one hand, reached down past him, grabbed a bottle and glass and with expert dexterity poured himself a large measure.

The barkeeper, a large, burly man, on being released, reached down for a shotgun, only to receive a smashing blow across the neck and shoulders with the bottle in Jed's hand.

The sudden commotion in the saloon aroused Bill Jones from the office on the first floor, and he moved towards the veranda which overlooked the saloon.

Bill Jones was the saloon owner and appeared to the townsfolk as a man not to be trifled with, particularly as he was always accompanied by Tom and Ben, two high-living, fast-shooting characters, who shot first then asked questions later.

Turning his head towards Tom, he said only one thing: "Go down and sort it out." Turning to Ben, he said, "Keep him covered."

"You heard the man," Tom said to Jed. "Get out."

"Are you talking to me, friend," said Jed.

First of all, I ain't no friend of a sawn-off black; and secondly, if you don't go you will go to your funeral." Simultaneously he moved his right hand towards his holster.

This movement set off a chain of events with something approaching the speed of light.

Jed lunged forward, grabbed Tom and spun him around to form a shield against the gun of Ben, which he had seen reflected in the mirror. His left hand at the same time had drawn his gun and pushed it into Tom's back. The situation was not quite stalemate as by this time Jed had pushed Tom slightly forward and drawn his other gun. In the same movement he fired the gun at Ben on the balcony. He hit him on the hand and his gun went spinning through the air. Ben grasped his wrist with his face twisted in agony.

Jed called out, "One move from you or anybody else in this room and this guy will get his lot, for sure."

"Serve the guy properly," said Jones. "Set a bottle on my table and join me," he said to Jed, thinking at the same time that this guy could be used to his advantage.

The barkeeper was rubbing his sore head, and somewhat enjoying the whisky which was still trickling down his face.

"You heard what I said."

With that, the barkeeper snatched a bottle of the best and took it over to Bill Jones' table.

Jed released Tom, but kept his gun trained on him until he reached the table, where he holstered the gun and sat down. Picking up the glass, he drank the whisky. Jed thought that Redwood City left a lot to be desired, so he decided to leave and seek his fortune elsewhere and not get involved with the locals as he wished to avoid any problems with various landowners.

Chapter Two

Colonel Walter Constant was a former Southern army man, six feet six inches tall, heavily built with grey hair. He had lost his left hand during the civil war and had an iron fist as a substitute. He had the biggest ranch spread in the county and lived alone as his wife had died some years ago. His only relative was his daughter, Val Constant, who was twenty-five years old, attractive with auburn hair. She was an excellent horsewoman, but she had left the city some while ago. Colonel Constant's great friend of many years' standing was Sheriff Eddy Moredon, who dispensed law and order in Redwood City and nobody really worried how he did it.

Redwood City itself was a harbour for a great number of notorious characters who had had several brushes with the law in many states. Here in the town law-breakers got away with most things; however, nobody had actually killed anybody for a long while, so generally the average citizen did not seem to worry.

Sheriff Eddy, however, was an old man. He had seen service in the civil war, being captured, but he was not treated with the respect he felt he deserved by the townsfolk. He was dying of a wasting disease, and his graveyard cough had become very severe over the last few years. His discomfort was only added to by his incessant smoking. He knew he was dying and put the entire blame on the privations he suffered during his prisoner-of-war days. It caused great problems to Colonel Constant, who wanted to keep his friendship with the sheriff while, at the same time, making very sure that on his demise nothing would change.

Reflecting back on the past, the Colonel recalled another good friend from his army days – Major Westwood, who was now in some way connected with the Legal Department in Turio. Major Westwood was responsible for providing law-enforcement officers throughout the land, and the Colonel thought he would pay him a visit to see if he could suggest anybody for the job, which would very shortly be available. However, it transpired that the only candidate at present was a fully qualified individual by the name of Jedassai Vincent Coogan. Major Westwood did not mention at this stage that this man, Jed, had saved his life on two occasions during the civil war, even though he was on the opposite side.

Colonel Constant decided that with a name like Jedassai he must be a gentleman, and consequently he would be able to mould him into his own ways. So without more ado he almost insisted that this Jedessai Vincent Coogan should be drafted to Redwood City immediately after the demise of Sheriff Moredon.

The day eventually arrived: the Sheriff drew his last breath and was laid to rest with a ceremony that befitted a man of his rank. Immediately Colonel Constant advised Major Westwood of the situation and received a telegram to say, 'Coogan appointed Marshal of Redwood City on 31 July. Westwood.' Preparations were made to welcome this fine Southern gentleman, who was to become marshal of the city. All the storekeepers and any who mattered were advised that the new marshal was arriving on the 31st.

When the appointed day at 5 p.m. arrived, a five-foot-six-inch stocky black man with a crew cut stepped out of the train and the word 'MARSHAL' stuck out like a searchlight from the badge on his breast. Marshal Coogan made his way towards the Colonel. Coogan knew the area and, apart from being a reformed character, he was an excellent gunman.

Constant appeared quite uninterested. He was more concerned about the arrival of his daughter the following day. With a disdainful look, he completely ignored the Marshal and rode off. Everybody who was anyone was talking about the eagerly awaited return of Val Constant, the daughter of the Colonel. She had left Redwood City some five years ago in somewhat of a cloud, but nobody really knew the truth. One day she was an attractive twenty-year-old flaunting herself around the town; the next day she had disappeared off to a finishing school.

Word had got back, as invariably it does, that Val had met a newspaper man named Justin Vine and eloped with him, only for her to be tracked down by her rich father and his hired help. The newspaper man had to disappear – so the story went.

∗∗∗

The day had arrived when she was returning home, and all appeared to be forgiven. The Colonel had arranged a civic reception for his daughter, and was no doubt looking forward to the reunion excitedly. The train was due to arrive at 11 a.m. and at ten thirty the Colonel arrived with his ranch manager. Apart from those men, the station was deserted. The only road to the station was through the main street, and almost the entire population were in the saloons or stores just waiting to catch their first glimpse of Val Constant.

Marshal Jed Coogan left his office and climbed slowly on to his horse. Then he rode to the station with the intention of meeting the train, collecting the mail and answering any questions the train officials might have. On his arrival at the station he hitched his horse to the rail, sauntered to the booking hall, leaned on the wall, adjusted his Stetson and rolled himself a cigarette. The time was about ten fifty-five.

The silence was broken by the noise of the engine, clearly advising everybody that it was on schedule. The driver did not intend hanging around at Redwood City. The train pulled into the station, and at that precise moment Jed stepped on to the platform, as did the Colonel. Their eyes met in anger. Jed averted his suddenly as a vision descended from the carriage. She stumbled and missed the bottom step, and on sprinting forward he caught her in his powerful arms.

"Thank you, sir," said Val.

Before Jed had uttered a word he was roughly pushed aside by the Colonel and the ranch manager, Joe Stead.

Val was swept up in her father's arms and, having got over the initial shock of the reunion with her father, she stopped, turned her head and looked at Jed again. He was smiling. He could see nothing except this dark-haired, attractive young woman with smiling eyes and with a look of loneliness about her.

At this point Jed decided that it was now or never – or maybe not for a long time anyway – so he walked towards her and said, "Jed Coogan, Marshal of Redwood City, at your service, ma'am."

It was as if the earth stood still for Jed. She stood there and he knew deep down inside they would meet again and, he thought, preferably alone.

Joe Stead said, "Be off, Marshal. Miss Val has no time for the likes of you."

"I will be the judge of that," said Val.

The Colonel said nothing. His brow was extremely furrowed and he was thinking that things were going to be a bit difficult now.

Chapter Three

Luke Lestrange and Bud Guiden were sitting astride their horses, discussing a successful stagecoach robbery they had just completed. Although they had managed to collect some jewellery, they were very disappointed about the amount of cash obtained. So after a lot of thought they decided to get the rest of their gang and rob the great Pendle Bank in Redwood City. This would be no easy task as it was located next to the Sheriff's office and the local saloon. They decided to pay a visit to the local saloon and have a good look at any possibility.

On arrival in Redwood City, they had a bit of luck because when they tethered their horses they noticed that the wall between the stables and the bank was nothing more than heavy timber, and it appeared easy to gain access from the stables into the bank. And so the plan fell into place. When the stables closed in the evening they would enter through the wall into the bank.

When they reconnoitered the bank, they noticed, much to their amusement, that the safe was in view and the manager's door was open. It appeared to be a very easy safe to crack. Bud was quite an expert on safe breaking, and he had served a prison sentence for such an offence.

They decided it would be a piece of cake to rob this bank, and were further encouraged when they heard, whilst in the saloon, that the bank was holding considerable cash belonging to a rich cattle owner who had recently sold his herd. They made plans to rob the bank tomorrow evening when the saloon was closed.

Luke and Bud rounded up a gang of four, duly broke into the stables and into the bank, and with little effort they made their way into the manager's office, opened the safe and emptied it of $50,000 cash.

They were leaving the stables and just about to ride away when they were accosted by the teller, Joe Bletchley. A single gunshot rang out and the gang ran off. Strangely enough, it was a few minutes before the Marshal appeared, to be confronted by Joe, who managed to gasp that there were six men before dying. Jed realised the gang had a good start, but nevertheless he felt he had to try tracking them down.

He managed to pick up their trail and confronted two of the gang who were lagging being the main group. Shots were exchanged, and he was hit on his left shoulder and the two guys managed to escape. He decided to return to Redwood City, and as he rode slowly down the dusty street towards his office, his dust-covered stained shirt flapping in the slight breeze, his face grimaced with pain from the wounded shoulder. Blood was running down his left arm on to his faded blue jeans. He was all in after tracking the gang which had robbed the city bank and shot the teller, Joe Bletchley. He knew that the townsfolk were sorry to see him return even though he was in such a state.

As he rode by, curtains were drawn, faces peering around them and disappearing. It seemed like eternity as the door to his office drew nearer and nearer. He had hoped he would at least be able to make it with as much bearing as he usually had, but he knew it would be a supreme effort. However, he summoned up the effort needed and he reached the hitching rail in front of his office, sitting upright, his head held high. Then he casually dismounted, walked to the door of his office and literally fell in.

A feeling of nausea came over him, and before he could reach his bunk or chair he collapsed on the floor of his office, the door closing behind him.

He awoke sometime later, the perspiration dripping from his forehead, his arm throbbing with pain although the bleeding had stopped. He levered himself up and managed to struggle across to the chair. After a few minutes he dragged his weary body to the basin and poured some water into it. He tore off his bloodstained shirt and managed to wash his face and bloodstained arm. It appeared to be only a flesh wound. After he had cleaned it as well as he could, he bound his shoulder with part of the clean shirt, dusted himself down as well as he could, stumbled over to a chair and poured a cup of cold coffee from the pot on the stove. He sipped it slowly.

***

After a good night's rest he thought he would take some time out. He decided he would go and laze and perhaps have a swim on the edge of the river. He swam along beside the riverbank and was passing a large overhanging rock which hung over the corner where the river opened out. Then, hearing a sound, he stopped and climbed out of the water. Crouching behind a rock, to his amazement he saw the silhouette of a women in the shady cove walking towards the water, undoing her blouse buttons, slipping it off and dropping her jeans. She obviously had the same idea of cooling off on this hot, dusty day. She had dark hair and a trim figure with firm breasts, and walked with a lazy stride. She turned her head, and to his consternation he recognised it was Val Constant. What was she doing? He had some desire to rush towards her, and this began to overwhelm him because he knew he shouldn't. Deep in his heart he was aware of his lowly station – particularly that not only was he the wrong colour, but he was a lot older than her. So with regret he decided to leave. He resolved to creep back into the water and swim back to his clothes, hoping the circumstances would be different in another time and place.

He knew it was wrong, but he couldn't avert his gaze. He kept staring. He knew he was looking at a princely work of art which he wanted to possess, look at and hold in his arms. He was a hard-bitten man, but he was so moved that a tear ran down his face. Although she was in a different class, he realised in his heart he carried a torch which would never be extinguished, and he hoped that in the future an opportunity would cross his path.

***

The following day, Val Constant walked into the Marshal's office to talk to Jed, and her radiant presence was overwhelming. She sat in the chair in front of his desk.

"Good morning, ma'am," Jed said. "Are you well?"

"Yes," Val replied. "You asked me to call. What can I do for you?"

Jed could not take his eyes off her. As she crossed her legs, her skirt slipped and he caught a glimpse of her white tender thigh, which began to arouse the animal instinct in him. He wondered why a person should have such an effect on him and he could not stop thinking about it. He knew his mind should be on other things, such as organising a posse to try and trace the bank robbers, but all he could think of doing was walking over to the coffee pot, at the same time asking if she would like a cup of coffee. He also mentioned Joe Bletchley, who was shot in the bank raid.

It was not the coffee she was used to as it had been brewing for three days and therefore was an acquired taste, but she readily agreed and he poured the coffee. When he brought it to her he touched her arm, and he noticed that her hand was trembling as she accepted the cup, which made him wonder whether there was any mutual feeling. Dared he hope?

He decided once again it was time to ask about what he wanted to discuss. "Miss Constant," he said, thinking to himself this was not really what he wanted to talk about, "would it be possible to ask the Colonel for ten to twelve men to form a posse and try picking up the trail of the bank robbers?"

"Is that all you wanted to ask me?" she said.

He felt a warm glow and was slightly taken aback.

"I would like to start as soon as possible," he said, still wondering what she meant by her comment. Another time, when he was not under so much pressure, he might have said, "I would like to escort you home." But instead he said, "Yes ma'am. Thank you. I hope the men will come later."

With that, Val Constant walked out of the office feeling slightly bemused, thinking, 'Did he get me there just to ask that? He could easily have written out a message and asked for it to be passed to my father. She thought the way he handled it was sad. She also thought she detected a gleam of hope in his eyes. 'Why did I tremble when he touched my arm?' she asked herself.

She heard a rifle shot in the distance and thoughts of Jed went completely out of her mind. Without more ado she went towards her home. When she arrived she started thinking again. She spoke to her father regarding the posse, and he said that he could probably organise something. She decided that as there could be a little delay she could go down to the Marshal's office and tell him. She was secretly hoping that something might happen between them.

***

She went there early the following morning, and as she entered the room he was reclining on the bed, partially covered by a thick blanket. She could see he had virtually nothing on and appeared to be asleep. She wondered whether she should wake him or just climb on to the edge of the bed and see what would happen. However, before she could make up her mind he opened his eyes and looked at the beautiful woman standing silhouetted against the open door. And through her dress he realised once again what an amazing figure she had and how he wanted to hold her.

To his amazement she walked towards him smiling, her bosom heaving as she saw his emotions stirring. He got off the bed, wrapped in a blanket, realising he was almost naked, but he thought, 'So what?' He wanted her and he believed she wanted him.

Before he could utter a word, she stepped out of her dress and threw her arms around him, causing the blanket to fall. She looked at him and gasped with excitement. They kissed passionately and fell on the bed in each other's arms.

Val Constant's foreman had followed Val and wondered where she was going. He saw her enter the Marshal's office and followed her in. Jed was concerned as his gun was lying on a chair near the bed and he couldn't reach it. The foreman decided that this was the end of Jed – presumably on the instructions of Colonel Constant. Just as he was about to shoot Jed, Val threw herself in front of him and took the bullet in her left leg, at which Jed managed to leap across the room, pick up his gun and shoot the foreman dead. He looked at Val and saw that fortunately the bullet had just scratched her left leg and hardly left a mark, so they both dressed quickly, ran out of the office and rode off, wondering what the future would bring.

Chapter Four

Jed and Val decided they would get away from the area very quickly. Her father was a powerful man and had friends everywhere. Colonel Constant would leave no stone unturned in order to get his daughter back and at the same time somehow dispose of Marshal Jed. After all, Val was the heir to his vast estate and ranch; and whilst he would be prepared to forgive her, there was no way he would allow his ranch to be run by a black man. Jed and Val rode away in the direction of Leyton, which was only a few miles away, and booked into the local saloon, The Hanging Rock. Val was concerned about her father, so she sent a telegram – saying she was sorry about leaving, but she was well and would be in touch as soon as possible.

Things took a turn for Val when she received a message to say that her father had had a severe heart attack and was at death's door, so she persuaded Jed to let her go back to see her father before it was too late.

They rode back to the ranch, and Val was just in time to see her father. Despite being at death's door, he forgave Val and hoped she would return to run the ranch. He said he had left everything to her.

After a few hours he drew his last breath and quietly slipped away. Val was his only remaining relative, so naturally Val organised the funeral for her father, which virtually the whole town attended.

After the funeral a local lawyer, Jake Parkin, called to confirm to Val that she was the sole beneficiary under her father's will and would inherit the entire ranch. Of course she wanted to run the ranch, but needed a strong man to assist her. She thought long and hard and finally decided to get Jed to come and hopefully assist in the management of the ranch. This she did and he came back. The whole town accepted Jed as the ranch manager, but he felt he had to prove himself, apart from being a fast gunslinger. It was a daunting task for him, but he felt that because of his love for Val he had to knuckle down and run the ranch and try and expand it.

His first goal was to gain the confidence of the thirty-odd ranch hands, which was not easy as most of them were loyal to the late Colonel Constant and were apprehensive of this new man. Naturally they were hesitant about obeying his orders. So trouble was no doubt on the horizon.

Jen and Val were very much in love, so they decided to get married. They organised a very quiet affair, but much to their amazement the whole town turned up and all had a great time.

In an effort to get the ranch hands on his side, Jed and Val decided to give each of the ranch hands his own horse and saddle and a small share of the ranch in the form of a cooperative, in the hope that it would make them feel part of the ranch. Jed called a meeting and he and Val put the proposal to them. To his satisfaction they all unanimously agreed. To make it legal he decided to talk to the lawyer, who drew up a contract for each ranch hand who agreed to pay a dollar for his share. They divided twenty per cent of the company up so that each of the twenty hands would have a share. The remaining eighty per cent of the ranch was left in the ownership of Jed and Val, so they retained overall control. An inventory of the livestock was made and any profit made during the year was divided fairly. All the ranch hands agreed.

So Court Line Enterprises Ltd was formed and became very successful. The ranch went from strength to strength over the next five years, although during this time cattle rustling took place. Over fifty head of cattle disappeared, but Jed, with his previous experience as a marshal, with his friend the new marshal, Karl Fodden, after some weeks managed to track down the gang. Much to Jed's surprise, two of the rustlers turned out to be members of the gang who robbed the bank in Redwood City some while ago and shot Joe Benchley.

Marshal Fodden, with Jed's assistance, made sure the rustlers were in prison while awaiting trial in the not too distant future.

***

Shortly after this Jed and Val decided to start a family and a son was born. They named him Zeka.

Everything was running smoothly, so they decided to expand the cattle side of the business. To do this they had to find more water, so they decided to dig a number of trial boreholes in an area known as Deadhills Valley. Much to their surprise, after a number of attempts, they struck what they thought was water, but it was a rusty colour and didn't look as though it was safe to drink. Then one of the ranch hands said it looked like 'muddy oil', and Jed's immediate reaction was to tell everybody to keep it quiet; at the same time he went to the telegraph office and contacted a friend who was involved in an oil company.

Johnty Biggs arrived at the ranch with an oilman who confirmed it was oil. He recommended a further series of boreholes, and to Val and Jed's surprise it transpired that their land lay over a rich vein of oil. Before going any further it was necessary to make some arrangements with an oil company in order to exploit the situation.

After lengthy discussions, a deal was finally agreed with Brexit Star Oils Ltd. If the amount of oil expected proved to be correct, the future of Court Line Enterprises Ltd was guaranteed, and the twenty ranch hands and their families would all benefit.

After a period of time, oil wells were developed. The future of Val and Jed and the ranch hands was definitely secure.

Later, however, Val and Jed received a telegram from the managing director of Brexit Star Oils, saying he was coming to visit the oil wells as they appeared very successful.

Some two weeks later, Brexit Star Oils officials arrived, and when Val opened the door she was amazed to find the managing director was Justin Bryan, a face from the past (her first love) driven away by her late father. During the next few minutes Justin explained that he was shot and left for dead, but survived with extreme care from an Indian tribe; and eventually he had been able to make his way home to his parents, who owned the oil company. On the death of his father some while ago, he inherited the company. Naturally, he was very keen to help Val and Jed.

Val was overjoyed to see him, but this left her with a problem. After all, she was now very successful and happily married with a son, and another baby on the way.

Over a long dinner, events of the past were discussed and Justin Bryan also said he was happily married with a family of two daughters, and his wife, Eleanor, was also a major factor in the oil company. So it was decided that they would become good friends again and meet regularly with their families.

So what of the future? Would their previous relationship be renewed? Only time would tell.

Picture Gallery

Stormy Mountains

Still Water

Monet Bridge

Sunset Haven

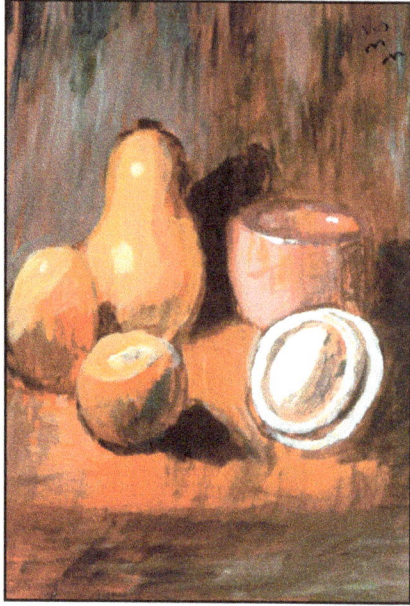

Roberto Replica

Roaring Success

Highcliff Villas

Maori Chief

After Lockdown

Zighand

Reunited?

Stained-Glass Window

Puffin Billie

Man Cave

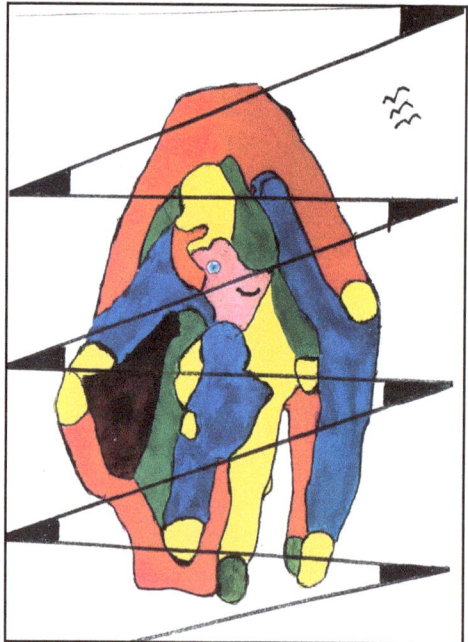

Imagine a house built on a hill – a house of ill-repute with a red light over the door. There is one man running up the hill, one man running down the hill, one man in the house and one man in a helicopter hovering over the house. What nationalities are they?

The first man, him Russian; the second man, him Finnish; the third man, Himalaya; and the fourth man, in the helicopter, him Irish waiting for the red light to turn green.

Remember sex is not the answer.

"Sex?" is the question; "Yes" is the answer.

Are falsies the bust that money can buy?

THE MOST SATISFYING WAY TO LIVE LIFE IS AT THE JUNCTION OF ORDER AND CHAOS.

Two actors on tour were staying in a B & B for two weeks. They both liked a glass of sherry every night, but noticed that when they arrived home the level of sherry in the bottle had gone down. This went on for some nights. They were upset, so took the bottle to the toilet and filled it up, but every night the level still went down. They were so amazed, but said nothing. On their departure they thanked the landlady, having had a good time, and said they hoped she enjoyed the sherry.

"Oh, my dear sirs," she said, "I don't drink, but I always put some in your trifle every night!"

A vicar during a sermon about morals said, "It starts with the first cigarette, and leads to a glass of whisky, then to the first immoral woman."

A voice from the back of the church said, "Where can I buy those cigarettes?"

WHY ARE YOU YOUNG AT HEART, BUT OLDER IN OTHER PLACES?

An eminent politician visiting an old people's home said to a resident, "Do you know who I am?"

"No," came the reply, "but ask at reception – they will be able to tell you!"

Speaking at a dinner, the speaker was very nervous, beginning, "I conceive – I conceive – I conceive –"

A member of the audience called out, "Mr Speaker, you have conceived thrice and brought forth nothing!"

Two old ladies are talking.

"Do you remember the minuet?" says one.

"Oh dear," says the other, "I don't even remember who I slept with!"

Waiter: "Would you like an aperitif, sir?"

Customer: "No, thanks. I always use my own teeth!"

IF YOU HAVE TIME TO SPARE, TRAVEL BY AIR.

THE MEASURE OF WHO WE ARE IS WHAT WE DO WITH WHAT WE HAVE!

Bottoms Up!

GROWING OLD ISN'T SO BAD WHEN YOU CONSIDER THE ALTERNATIVE.